OUR WORLD IN COLOR

JAPAN

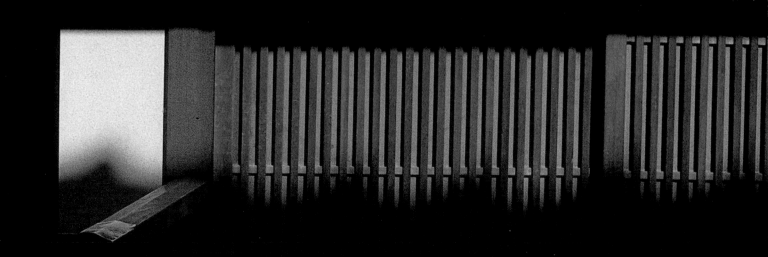

OUR WORLD IN COLOR JAPAN

Photography by Ken Straiton
Text by Peter Popham

The Guidebook Company Limited

Distributors

Australia and New Zealand: The Book Company,
100 Old Pittwater Road, Brookvale, NSW 2100, Australia.

Canada: Prentice Hall Canada,
1870 Birchmount Road, Scarborough, Ontario MIP 257,
Canada.

Hong Kong: China Guides Distribution Services Ltd.,
14 Ground Floor, Lower Kai Yuen Lane, North Point, Hong Kong.

India and Nepal: UBS Publishers' Distributors Ltd.,
5 Ansari Road, Post Box 7015, New Delhi 110 002, India.

Singapore and Malaysia: MPH Distributors (S) PTE Ltd.,
601 Sims Drive, No. 03/07-21, Pan-I Complex, Singapore 1438.

UK: Springfield Books Limited,
Springfield House, Norman Road, Dendy Dale,
Huddersfield HD8 8TH, West Yorkshire, England.

USA: Publishers Group West Inc.,
4065 Hollis, Emeryville, CA 94608, USA.

Text and captions by Peter Popham

Photography by Ken Straiton

Edited by Lesley Clark and Ralph Kiggell
An A to Z of Fun Facts by Mary Cooch

Designed by Joan Law Design & Photography
Cover colour separations by Sakai Lithocolour
Colour separations by Rainbow Graphic Arts Co., Ltd.
Printed in Hong Kong
by Toppan Printing Company (HK) Limited
ISBN 962-217-104-4

Title Spread
The frontage of a town house in Gion, the geisha quarter of Kyoto, expresses the sombre, mellow elegance of the old capital.

Right
Thatch, for centuries the most popular roofing material in many parts of the countryside, has fallen into disuse in modern times due to the expense and difficulty of upkeep and the cost of fire insurance. These fine old thatched farmhouses are among the many collected together at Takayama in Gifu Prefecture, in the Minzoku Mura (Folk Village) there. Takayama is located in the yukiguni (snow country) in the west of Honshu, an area which receives abundant snowfall every winter.

Pages 6-7
A major intersection in Ginza, playground of Tokyo's leisured classes for at least a century and still the capital's most expensive shopping and dining area.

Pages 8-9
Many traditional craftsmen still pursue their ancestral trades amidst the frenzy of change. This man in the working-class Asakusa section of Tokyo, formerly one of the most popular entertainment districts, is making cakes stuffed with sweet azuki bean paste.

Pages 10-11
Autumn colours at Kiyomizu Temple in Kyoto. Autumn is the prettiest season, and Japanese are avid viewers of the koyo, the autumn foliage. The delicate leaves of the momiji, the Japanese maple, shown here, turn a particularly gorgeous hue.

Pages 12-13
Images of Japan, among them the flapping koinobori (carp streamers) hoisted on high poles for Children's Day, 5 May; the 'comma' patterns on a shrine drum; o-mikuji (fortune-telling papers), left behind in the shrine ground because their auguries were negative; the strings of a koto; and incense burning before a temple.

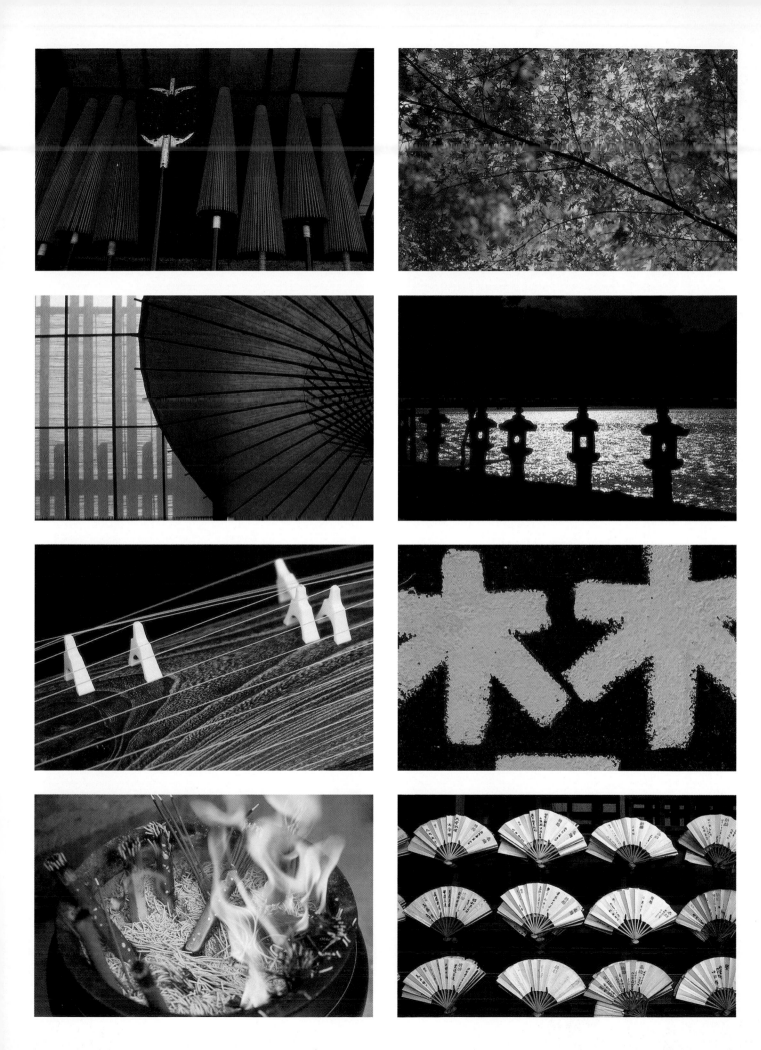

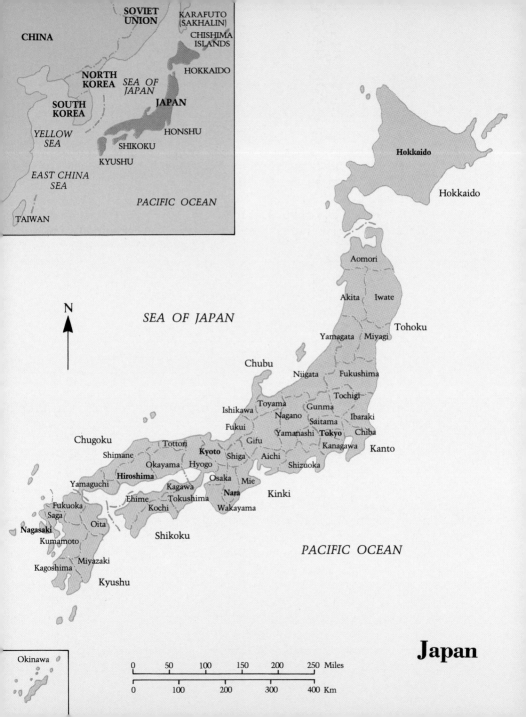

CHINA

SOVIET UNION

KARAFUTO (SAKHALIN)

CHISHIMA ISLANDS

NORTH KOREA

HOKKAIDO

SEA OF JAPAN

SOUTH KOREA

JAPAN

YELLOW SEA

HONSHU

SHIKOKU

KYUSHU

EAST CHINA SEA

PACIFIC OCEAN

TAIWAN

N

SEA OF JAPAN

Hokkaido

Hokkaido

Aomori

Akita | Iwate

Tohoku

Yamagata | Miyagi

Chubu

Niigata | Fukushima

Tochigi

Toyama | Gunma

Ishikawa | Nagano | Saitama | Ibaraki

Fukui | Yamanashi | **Tokyo** | Chiba

Gifu | Kanagawa | Kanto

Kyoto | Shiga | Aichi

Chugoku | Tottori | Shizuoka

Shimane | Okayama | Hyogo | Osaka | Mie

Hiroshima | Kagawa | **Nara**

Yamaguchi | Ehime | Tokushima | Wakayama | Kinki

Fukuoka | Kochi

Saga | Shikoku

Nagasaki | Oita

Kumamoto | *PACIFIC OCEAN*

Kagoshima | Miyazaki

Kyushu

Okinawa

0	50	100	150	200	250	Miles
0	100	200	300	400	Km	

Japan

INTRODUCTION

IF YOU WERE THE GREAT ARCHITECT, casting around for a place to erect a world-beating, world-leading civilization, it is unlikely that your gaze would settle for long on the islands of Japan.

Spattered across the ocean east of China, like hunks of bread thrown for the ducks, they are definitively peripheral: it was a slog from here to almost anywhere in the days before the jet. Though not insignificant in area, roughly one and a half times the size of Britain, they are largely uninhabitable. Steep, forested mountains dominate the interior, deterring from intimacy all but the monkeys and the mountain mystics. Japan's people cram themselves into the scraps of land, mostly along the coast, that are flat.

Even here, they are victims of the elements. Every year the Japanese archipelago is raked by typhoons causing frequent death and destruction. Yet more common and more feared are the earthquakes: Japan is one of the most seismically perilous corners of the world. In Tokyo, and many other places, minor tremors occur daily, while monster quakes demolish whole towns and cities often enough for the timing and location of the next 'Big One' to be a subject of lively debate. Tokyo and Yokohama were last reduced to rubble in 1923. Their next date with disaster is expected any time now.

Japan is no Promised Land; no milk and honey flow here. But it can be said that nature's gifts have proved, in the very long run, to be nicely balanced. Rigours of terrain and climate have instilled in the Japanese a fantastic capacity for work, and an ungrudging recognition of its necessity. Frugality, ingenuity and team-work are the hallmarks of a people unable to pluck their livelihood from the land.

The Japanese awareness of disaster and death, sharpened by the insights of Taoism and Buddhism, has produced a unique aesthetic sense: a devotion to phenomena of nature, such as the cherry blossom, the dewdrop, the full moon, the autumn grasses, the crying of insects, whose ephemeral beauty has a special, sharp poignancy because it is transient.

But the single factor that has most influenced Japan's development has been its distance from the continent: it is four times the distance from Dover, in England, to Calais, in France, at the very closest point. Although too far away to be successfully invaded, as Khublai Khan discovered, it was still close enough to fall deeply under the influence of the Chinese civilization. Brave envoys and scholars of the early centuries of the Christian era travelled to China and returned with everything the inhabitants had to teach. In sharp contrast to other satellites of China, such as Korea, Japan was distant enough to remove itself from the Chinese shadow when the country began to stagnate. This independence allowed it to turn to face the opposite direction and begin to learn from the West.

Out of this perfect balance with China, a civilization arose in Japan that was highly peculiar, in both senses of the word. The country was indebted to China for practically every amenity of life and every achievement of the intellect, from chopsticks to Confucianism. Yet in its centuries of seclusion, Japan put each import through a 'sea change'. And 'rich and strange', indeed, were the emerging transformations, which lost their foreignness and became distinctly Japanese.

The forms, devices and customs borrowed from the West in the last 120 years have been put through a similar process of transmutation but, in keeping with the 20th century, the whole process has been very much more frenzied!

Where the Japanese originally came from is a matter of dispute. Racially, they are of the same Mongolian stock as the Chinese and Koreans; probably their first ancestors moved into the archipelago from the continent while there was still a land bridge connecting them. Grammatical similarities suggest an ancient link with the Koreans, Japan's nearest neighbours. The Chinese and Japanese languages, by contrast, are poles apart. Cultural manifestations, notably the indigenous post-and-beam architecture, suggest a prehistoric link with Southeast Asia or Polynesia but it has never been clearly substantiated.

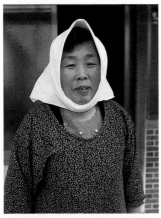

In the old village of Tsumago, a stop on the back way from Kyoto to Tokyo in the old days, the Tokugawa Period mood is preserved in the ancient architecture — and some of the local people (top) help the illusion along by wearing period costume. The red logo on this man's hat is modern and signifies the postal service. Most Japanese postmen dress more conventionally (above).

The Japanese only learned to write from the Chinese in the early centuries of the Christian era, so developments before that are rather vague. According to myth, Japanese civilization began in the island of Kyushu, when a descendant of the sun goddess came down to earth and initiated the dynasty of emperor-shamans that has led, in an unbroken line, to the present incumbent, Akihito — supposedly number 125.

Whatever truth may lie behind the myth, the scholarly consensus is that the cradle of early Japanese civilization was in the Yamato area, near Nara, in the western part of the main island of Honshu. Here, in this relatively broad and fertile inland plain, the first cities grew, and the civilization gradually began to assume a recognizably Japanese form.

Here it was, in the sixth and succeeding centuries, that the first Japanese masterpieces of Buddhist art were erected, including temples, such as Todaiji with its heroic Buddha image. Chinese concepts of government were introduced, though crucially modified to harmonize with prevailing Japanese practice. The Chinese notion of an emperor influenced the way the Japanese felt about their own ruler, for example, and they gave him a title, *tenno*, which had a decidedly Chinese ring to it. But they balked at importing the idea that he ruled by a mandate from heaven. As Chinese history has frequently demonstrated, that mandate can be withdrawn from a ruler whose popularity plummets low enough, and the result is a violent change of dynasty. Japan's imperial house, in contrast, was itself divine, and could therefore never be replaced.

In a similar way, the importation of Buddhism and its patronage by the ruling class did not result in the eclipse of the primitive animistic religion which was there already. Eastern religions are more tolerant than Christianity or Islam: after something of a struggle, Buddhism and Shinto (the Way of the Gods), as the native religion had come to be called, found a way to lie down together, and they have just about managed to co-exist ever since.

Nearly all Japanese are both Shintoists and Buddhists. Buddhism, the deep, rather dark, philosophical religion whose basic tenets are the helplessness of man and the inevitability of suffering, governs Japanese rites of death, and the communion with dead ancestors in festivals, such as the summer Obon. Shinto lacks all pretensions to philosophy. It straightforwardly celebrates life, expresses awe in the face of all potent phenomena, be they waterfalls, volcanoes or great generals, and regards death as just one of many types of contamination. It's to Shinto that Japanese turn when they wish to sanctify births or marriages, purify the sites of their houses, or get divine help in passing exams or acquiring more money.

Recognizing that the average Japanese finds no difficulty in accommodating these radically different religions in his mind and life is an important step towards understanding these enigmatic people.

Nara was Japan's first permanent capital — previously the capital was shifted each time an emperor died — and its first real urban centre, with a population of some 200,000. But its pre-eminence was short-lived: in 794, just a century after its foundation, the imperial seat was shifted north to Heian, later renamed Kyoto, where it was to remain for more than a thousand years.

The first 400 years of Kyoto's history are called the Heian (peace) Period, and these were the most glorious. It was, indeed, an era of peace and relative prosperity, when the questions of who was to govern the nation and how seemed to have been settled once and for all. It was also the period when Japan first tasted the sweetness of cultural emancipation from China. Within the privileged confines of the imperial court, many of the qualities that the world still thinks of today as distinctly Japanese were distilled and perfected. Formality, politeness, adherence to rigid notions of hierarchy and rigid rules of behaviour, on the one hand; intense lyricism, a passionate if rather over-precious sympathy for the beauty and sadness of nature, on the other; these were the achievements of the Heian court. The lyricism spawned a school of courtly love poetry which anticipated England's Elizabethans by some 500 years. A stultifying, in-turned world, it nonetheless produced the world's first novel, Murasaki Shikibu's *The Tale of Genji*, and many other lasting works of prose and verse.

The court's self-absorption was finally its undoing. While the courtiers held charming incense-identifying contests and wooed their mistresses to the plucking of the *koto*, the benighted provinces were stirring. Clans of warriors were dispatched to control them, and, as they succeeded in the task, they came gradually to usurp the power of their imperial rulers.

First the Taira clan asserted its dominance over the effete court, but they were skillfully bought out by the marriage of the clan leader to the daughter of a Fujiwara, the most prominent family in the country after the emperor's.

Next was the turn of the Taira's great rivals, the clan of Minamoto. Sprung from the rough and uncultivated east of the country — the Kanto, site of present-day Tokyo — these fighting men were less susceptible to the perfumes and soft pillows of Kyoto, and in a decisive battle in 1192 they drove the Taira into the sea. Their leader, Yoritomo, established the first *bakufu* (military government) in the fishing village of Kamakura, now a pretty tourist town one hour south of Tokyo.

Yoritomo, the first shogun, was now Japan's unchallenged ruler, but what is interesting and very characteristic is that this did not tempt him to destroy the imperial court. Despite his rustic origins, he was careful to obtain the formal consent of the emperor to his rule and to treat the court with as great a show of respect and deference as they had demanded when they were genuinely powerful. In this way began the habits of mask-wearing and role-playing which have persisted in Japanese public life to the present day.

But Yoritomo and his successors introduced important new strands into the Japanese tapestry, summed up in the word *samurai*. Now the shogun was top dog, the martial skills of his warriors assumed a new importance, especially *kendo* (the way of the sword) and *kyudo* (the way of the bow). Under the influence of the Zen school of Buddhism, newly arrived from China and enthusiastically patronized by the shoguns, kendo and kyudo came to be seen as far more than methods of killing opponents. Like the main Zen activity, sitting meditation, they came to be regarded as ways of advancing spiritually — despite the death and destruction incurred.

The power of Kamakura was based on ties of loyalty linking the shogun with a fairly small number of feudal lords dotted around the country. As a structure of authority it was flimsy, and after its first real test it began to crumble.

The Mongol warlord Khublai Khan had already created a vast empire stretching from eastern Europe to China. Now, in 1274, for reasons that seem to have had more to do with megalomania than rational strategy, he tried to expand it to include Japan. Twice he sent invasion fleets to the shores of Kyushu, their soldiers armed with catapults and exploding fireballs and drilled to fight in organized units. The samurai, who were specialized in man-to-man combat, and were waiting for them on the shore, would have been no match for them. By amazing good luck, however, on both occasions typhoons sprang up and scattered the Mongolian ships and finally the invasion attempt was abandoned. The Japanese called the typhoons *kamikaze* (divine winds) and began to believe that their land was favoured by the gods and would never be conquered — the events of 1945 were a monumental shock.

The shogun's victory over the Mongols finally proved pyrrhic: the cost of raising a force to defend the country so drained his coffers and those of his dependent lords that, within a few decades, rival samurai had defeated them and Kamakura's moment of glory had passed.

Two and a half centuries of confusion ensued. A new line of shoguns, the Ashikaga, ruled nominally through these years but by the middle of the 15th century, their real power had dissipated and Japan was plunged into a century of provincial civil war. Against this background of chaos and bloodshed, however, extraordinary cultural advances were made.

Western dress is nearly universal now, even in the remote corner of the Sea of Japan coast where this lady (opposite centre) lives. In general, the kimono is reserved for special occasions, such as the visit to a Shinto shrine on Seijin-no-Hi (Coming of Age Day) on 15 January, and is worn by young women (top) who will reach the age of 20 during the year; and geisha (above), participating in the famous Sanja Festival in Asakusa, Tokyo.

Early autumn at a Kyoto temple. Many fabulously old ginkgo trees are found in the grounds of temples. In autumn they turn a dazzling shade of yellow.

A corner of Sofukuji Temple in Nagasaki, one of several Ming-style Chinese Buddhist temples in the city. This one dates from the early 17th century.

This was the period when the polite arts and graces of the upper class reached their peak of development. The haunting, mesmerisingly slow poetic drama, the Noh, was perfected, and so entranced the husky warlords of the time that battles were postponed so they could relish it to the full. The humble tea party was refined, codified and ritualized until it became *cha-no-yu*, the tea ceremony or 'Zen meditation for laymen', as it is sometimes described. Performed in tiny, rustic cottages specially built for the purpose, decorated with the severest simplicity — a single display of cut flowers, a hanging scroll with a picture or a verse painted on it — the ceremony consisted simply of the boiling of the water and the brewing, handing round and drinking of the tea. The art and the beauty lay in the calm, elegant manner in which these actions were performed. The busy warriors and merchants who participated considered it a balm to the soul.

A passionate sort of connoisseurship grew up around the tea ceremony. Wealthy men sought out exquisite examples of the vessels and implements used in it — the bamboo whisks used for beating the soupy, bitter green tea, the tea caddies, the iron kettles, the bowls, the flower vases — and paid small fortunes for the best ones. The obsession held everyone in its grip, right up to the shogun himself; one feudal lord facing the death sentence was pardoned when he made the shogun a timely present of a particularly choice tea caddy!

The value these men placed on objects of beauty helped pave the way for the Japanese connoisseurs of today, who do not hesitate to pay tens of millions of dollars for a single painting by Picasso or Van Gogh.

Down the centuries since the Heian Period, Japan's connection with the outside world had been restricted to an on-off relationship with China. Towards the end of the Muromachi Period, however, and indirectly hastening its end, there occurred a new and dramatic intrusion — the arrival of the Europeans!

The Portuguese arrived first, in 1542, their merchants followed rapidly by their missionaries, who initiated what later came to be called Japan's Christian Century. The Jesuits, led by Francis Xavier, had considerable success in winning the hearts and minds of feudal lords, especially in Kyushu, the island in which they landed. But more significant in the long run than the doctrines the Europeans brought with them were their firearms. The Japanese quickly grasped the usefulness of these, and artisans were soon hard at work, turning out magnificent imitations for the warring lords. When they were used in battle, they quickly ended the long stalemate between the warring fiefdoms.

Out of the gun smoke arose three generals, one after another, all from the central part of the country near present-day Nagoya. By the time they had finished with it, Japan had been transformed from a parcel of warring states into a single, unified entity. And so it was to remain.

The three giants were Oda Nobunaga, Toyotomi Hideyoshi and Tokugawa Ieyasu. Nobunaga, people like to say, quarried the stones, Hideyoshi shaped them and Tokugawa set them into place.

Typical of the new era was the development of official attitudes to the Christian missionaries. Nobunaga tolerated, even encouraged them. Hideyoshi, notorious for his impulsive cruelty and violence, issued an edict banishing them from the country but never put it systematically into effect. Then, with the accession of Ieyasu, persecution began in earnest. All foreigners were expelled, and some 6,000 Japanese Christians suffered hideous martyrdom for the alien faith. For the security of his regime, and to prevent further contamination by foreign 'barbarians', Ieyasu closed the country to practically all of the outside world. The only exceptions were a trickle of trade with China, and the setting up of a Dutch trading station on an artificial island in Nagasaki Bay. This allowed the shoguns an occasional glimpse of the civil and intellectual revolutions occurring on the other side of the world.

Countries that have closed their doors to the outside world in modern times, Burma say, or Albania, have quickly stagnated. Japan was on its own for nearly 250 years, yet it continued to develop. The deeply conservative men behind the Tokugawa regime nailed down the nation's social structure as rigidly as they could. They obliged the four tiers of society: samurai, farmers, artisans and merchants, to follow minutely prescribed dress codes and to live only in certain types of houses in particular neighbourhoods; intercourse between the classes was strictly taboo. But despite their efforts, the Tokugawa Period was one of rapid and fascinating change.

Dogged by decades of uninterrupted peace, the samurai, whose only real function was to fight, felt increasingly useless as the age advanced. The half-starved farmers, grossly overtaxed as usual, periodically rose up in anger to protest. But down at the bottom of the social scale, the merchants, as the only members of society who could use their wits to increase their earnings, enjoyed a phenomenal boost in their fortunes. Their prosperity found expression in new artistic forms of great charm and vitality, most famously the ukiyoe print and the kabuki theatre.

For all its artistry, there is a gloomy quality to much of Japanese art prior to these years. The old music has the melodic felicity of the wailing of the damned, to Western ears. The Noh theatre sends everyone to sleep, modern-day Japanese included. The old masters of poetry and the tea ceremony were careful to explain that the beauty they most valued was best described by the words 'cold' and 'withered'. Without the gaiety and élan of the bourgeois art of the Tokugawa Period, it is unlikely that Japanese aesthetics would ever have caught on in the West at all.

But here was something new: artists who, like their forbears, were fascinated, not grieved, by the ephemeral — by *ukiyoe*, the floating world. The breeding grounds of their inspiration were the pleasure quarters, sections like the Yoshiwara in Edo (Tokyo), cordoned-off areas where the iron rules of Tokugawa society could be temporarily forgotten, where samurai and merchant rubbed shoulders without ceremony and where the girls were abundant, available and extremely skilled!

In these nightless cities the new art was born: the pathetic love-suicide dramas of the puppet theatre, the dances of the kabuki, accompanied by the newly-imported, banjo-like *shamisen*, the woodblock prints of celebrated courtesans, all were part of the liberated and liberating fume of the times.

When the Tokugawa Period ended, Japan's modern age began. For the Western eye, Japanese art is defined by its utter peculiarity and its distance from our own experience. As soon as that 'alieness' starts to be diluted — as soon as the Japanese begin painting in oils, writing socialist-realist novels, building in brick and staging productions of Ibsen — we start to lose interest in a hurry. But Western interest in things traditionally Japanese has saved unique works of art from the rubbish dump.

Japan's modern era began formally in 1868, when the emperor, whose ancestors had been going through their cobwebbed and under-financed rituals in considerable obscurity for the preceding 700 years, was brought centre stage and made the figurehead of a New Japan. A fantastic project of assimilation got under way: everything up to date which the West had, Japan wanted, from lightning conductors to ballroom dancing, from mutton-chop whiskers to suspension bridges. Japan's special, unique past, so much prized by the Western intellectuals who came to the country after the doors swung open, was felt to be ripe for the scrapheap. Horyuji, for example, the magnificent Nara Period temple complex, parts of which are among the world's oldest wooden buildings, was sold as fuel to a public bath house, and only saved by the intervention of a Western scholar.

All Japan's energy was focused on learning, assimilating, imitating and adapting. Not surprisingly, results often looked mediocre and uninspired to Western eyes.

But that new beginning is more than 120 years in the past now. Within five years, Japan will celebrate the centenary of its stunning victory over the Russians which

Typically imposing image of the cosmic Buddha, Vairochana, known in Japanese simply as Daibutsu — Great Buddha (top). The Peace Memorial statue in Nagasaki (centre), erected at the epicentre of the nuclear explosion which devastated the city in August 1945. Wayside Buddhist images (above) in the old city of Kanazawa, on the Sea of Japan coast. The persistence of a spirit of Buddhist piety is attested by the clean bibs and offerings of fresh flowers.

heralded its arrival on the world stage as a power to be reckoned with. Industrialization, the brief flirtation with democracy in the '20s, the descent into militant nationalism and a disastrous war — all these milestones are receding rapidly into the past. The age of assimilation is over. Now it's Japan's peers and trading partners around the world who face the tough challenge of assimilating what Japan has achieved, in the form of industrial, technological and commercial know-how.

So modern Japan can claim a certain maturity. But what of the culture? There has, indeed, been a sad falling off; the ground lost in those early decades of the Meiji Period, when everything Japanese was considered worthless, everything Western admirable, has never been recovered. Among the dozens of exquisite images in this book, the truly modern examples are noteworthy only for their vulgarity, their gigantic scale, their grotesqueness — at the very best, their accidental beauty.

The neon and the tail lights of Ginza: amazing, yes, but only because more numerous or brighter than those of Times Square or Piccadilly Circus. The overview of Tokyo: staggeringly huge. The massed, shirt-sleeved clones of the stock exchange, like schoolboys in an enormous classroom. The foolish kitsch of Harajuku's '50s revivalists. The skyscrapers of Shinjuku: an artless, senseless jumble, reflecting, with unintended humour, the nearly identical jumble among the lower-rise buildings which cluster around their ankles.

The Japanese themselves are only too aware that there has been a decline, that the traditional arts have become fossilized, and that the new ones which have sprung up lack both the sincerity of the old and the power and integration of those of the West.

Japan is now the producer of the world's hardware *par excellence*: and its cars, videos, fax machines, cameras have become unrivalled in quality and design. But somewhere along the line, the Japanese have lost the wherewithal — the heart, the soul, the imagination, the conviction — to produce the software.

As wisdom comes with age and post-war Japan regains its footing and its confidence, one can only hope that this sad state of affairs will be remedied and that the arts of Japan will rise to their former heights of aesthetic excellence.

O-sembe (rice crackers) (top), *at a stall in Tokyo's Asakusa district. Bottles of* sake *(centre) and beer make acceptable offerings at Shinto holy places, such as here at the Meiji Shrine in Tokyo. Perfectly uniform (though tasteless) tomatoes (above) are one of the bonuses of the modernization of Japanese agriculture. A spacious restaurant takes up several storeys (right)*

The 50-storey-plus skyscrapers of Shinjuku (top), the capital's only skyscraper park, form a jumble which is as artless as that made by the smaller buildings which cluster around their ankles. Even when waiting for a train (centre), a kimono can lend a person poise. Taking the midday sun in Marunouchi (above), the old business section of central Tokyo which is dominated by Mitsubishi companies.

Left
A scramble-type crossing in Ginza.

Preceding pages
Tokyo, seen from one of the skyscrapers in the Shinjuku district, goes on forever. Close on 30 million people now inhabit the metropolitan area.

Above
Tokyo's stock exchange is the second largest in the world, with roughly half the total equity of Wall Street but a turnover which now rivals that of New York.

Right
A Babel of scripts on a main street in Ginza: romaji (roman script), the two types of Japanese kana script, as well as Chinese kanji.

Bright lights in the big city: another view of Ginza (left) ... And the whimsical exterior of a game parlour (top).

Above
A cheaper and homelier image is projected by this pub-cum yakitori (barbecued chicken) joint under the railway tracks near Ginza.

Above left
Dayglo typography is the hallmark of Akihabara, the electronics retailing centre of Japan, though, due to the high yen, a bargain basement no more.

Above
Central Tokyo is not all rip-off night-clubs. Most of the grilled meat and vegetable snacks served in this open-air restaurant cost little more than one pound sterling each.

Left and right
Rain puddles reflect Ginza's lights.

Huge poster (above) *advertising*
Bee-Bop High School, *one of
many recent films depicting the
antics of teenage punks.
Cinema-goers can finish up
with a meal, including
Kentucky Fried Chicken if they
wish* (right).

Left
*The Kabuki-Za in Ginza, one of
Tokyo's top kabuki theatres.
Performances start in the
morning and go on all day.*

Memorial to a paragon of
loyalty *(below right): once there
was a dog called Hachiko, who
went to Shibuya Station in
Tokyo each day to wait for his
master to come home from
work. One day his master
failed to come home because he
had died — but the dog
continued to wait for him, day
in, day out, until his fame
spread throughout Japan. When
Hachiko finally died, a statue
was erected outside Shibuya
Station to commemorate his
fidelity. The square in which it
sits is now Tokyo's most
famous meeting-place.*

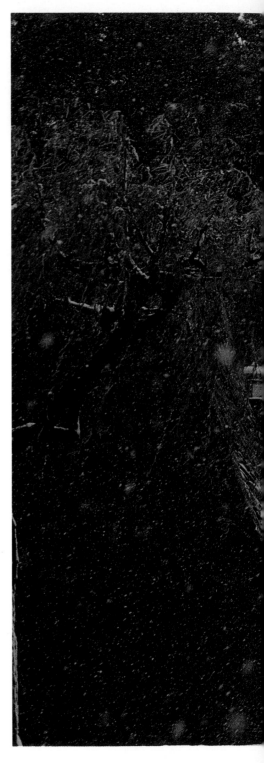

Above
Noren *(half-curtains) indicate a symbolic divide between inside and out. Hung up outside a traditional restaurant* (top left) *they mean it's open. Bamboo* sudare *(screens)* (below right) *ward off the sun.*

Right
The Nijubashi Gate of Tokyo's Imperial Palace in a rare winter snowstorm: classical castle architecture and Victorian bridge design are pleasingly harmonized.

A huge and shady park in the west of central Tokyo, Meiji Shrine, was laid out to commemorate Emperor Meiji, who reigned from 1868 to 1912. He was modern Japan's most revered monarch. Many day-to-day visitors come to this quiet area (above and left) to rest, or even to attend weddings (far right) which are often held at Shinto shrines and blessed by Shinto priests.

The details of the shrine are worth a closer look.

This unpainted torii (entrance gate) (top right) to the shrine is decorated with a gold chrysanthemum, the imperial flower. Elsewhere there are huge drums (centre) with fine surface detail, and a variety of ritual implements (below right).

Far and centre left
Young Shinto priests at Meiji Shrine.

Left
Shrine offerings of o-mochi (glutinous rice cakes).

Above
Traditional dance at Meiji Shrine.

Above
In the Shichi-go-san (7-5-3) festival in November, girls of seven, boys of five and three-year-olds of both sexes are dressed in traditional finery and paraded to major shrines to be blessed.

Left
Millions of Japanese visit Shinto shrines at New Year to buy a good luck arrow (returning the one bought the year before) and to check on prospects for the year ahead as predicted by the o-mikuji (fortune-telling) papers on sale in the shrine grounds.

Scenes from Sanja Matsuri, plebeian Tokyo's great traditional celebration held every May. The focus of this — as of most such festivals — is the o-ikoshi *(portable shrine) borne aloft by virile young men.*

Ritualized displays of archery are among the performances that can be witnessed at Tokyo's Meiji Shrine on Coming-of-Age Day in mid-January . . .

. . . While only minutes away in Harajuku, rock'n rollers find various ways to celebrate their youthfulness.

Cherry-blossom viewing at Chidori-ga-fuchi in central Tokyo.

Right
Above, the Shinkansen (bullet train) speeds towards Osaka from Tokyo at 209 kmph (130 mph); underneath, the cheap and tiny bars frequented by local sarariman (white-collar workers).

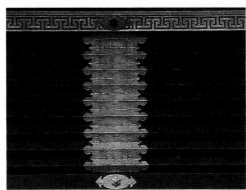

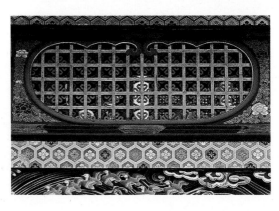

The natural beauty of Nikko in the mountains north of Tokyo, draws many from the capital at weekends. Here is the site of the Toshogu Shrine, the gorgeously decorated mausoleum of the first Tokugawa shogun, Ieyasu, and his grandson.

Above
The shrine of Hachiman, the Shinto deity of war, was built at Kamakura by Yoritomo, the first Kamakura shogun.

Left
The Great Buddha of Kamakura, one of Japan's largest at 11 metres (37 feet) high and one of its most beautiful monuments.

Above
Wayside Buddhas before Mount Fuji, Japan's highest and most celebrated peak.

Right
Women make offerings to the Buddhist deity Jizo for the souls of infants lost through miscarriage or abortion.

Above
In the forests of Nagano, the 'roof of Japan'.

Left
Some countrywomen still wear garments like these of handwoven cotton, dyed indigo.

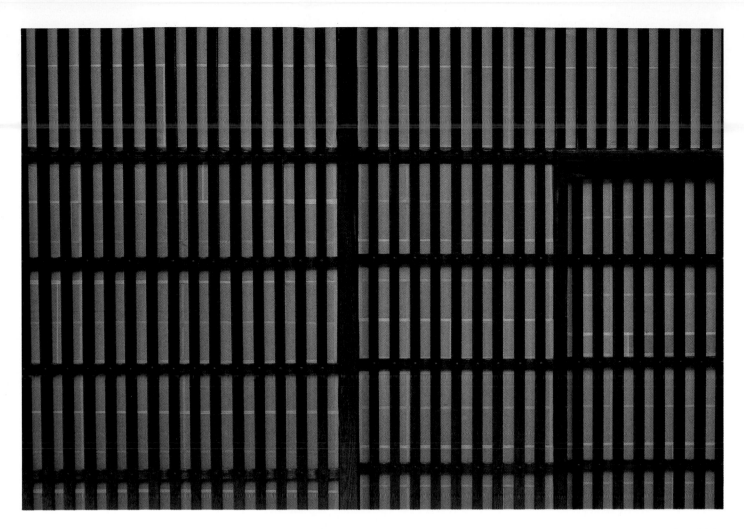

Above
House front in Narai, one of the villages of Nagano that has preserved its traditional look.

Right
Misty trees near the summit of Mt Ontake, Nagano.

Above
Sunlight streams into the elegant living room of a distinguished old ryokan *(inn) in Tsumago, Nagano Prefecture. Inns like this in Tsumago and in the nearby villages of Narai and Magome, were used by samurai in the Tokugawa Period on their way from Kyoto to Edo (Tokyo) along the 'back route'.*

Specimen of traditional weaving and dyeing at a folkart museum in Takayama (left), and wherewithal of the weaver's trade (right).

Winter in Takayama, in the mountains of Nagano. In February, during the festival of Setsubun, children throw beans to expel demons, symbolized by the bewigged red figure (below centre).

Below right
Hot spa in Gifu Prefecture in central Japan, open all the year round.

Above and left
Snow is a winter way of life in Fukui Prefecture on the Sea of Japan coast.

Above
Waxed-paper umbrellas help to keep off snow and rain.

Right
When the snow comes the menfolk head for the big cities to find seasonal work ... But some stay behind and play pachinko *(pinball) instead!*

Left and above
Binding stalks after the rice harvest. The stubble makes a comfortable seat for the children.

Top
Heavy, safe door-like shutters of an old wattle-and-daub kura *(storehouse). All houses of substance in the old days had a kura where family heirlooms could be stored away from the threat of fire.*

Top centre and right
The famous pine tree-covered islets of Matsushima, near Sendai in northern Honshu, are customarily described as one of Japan's 'three most beautiful sights'. The fishing boats (above centre), *however, are from Aomori Prefecture, in the extreme north of Honshu.*

Above
This pagoda at Kyoto's Kiyomizu temple, has been recently restored.

Left
The Kitano Temmangu Shrine also in Kyoto, has survived for a relatively long period.

Top
*City view from Kiyomizu Temple, with
Kyoto Tower at left.*

Right
A tunnel of torii *at Fushimi Inari Shrine in
Kyoto.*

Shinto shrines are common sights all over Japan. Some of the most beautiful are in the old court capital of Kyoto. The Heian Shrine (top left and right), *for example, is in Kyoto. It is a late-19th century reproduction on a reduced scale of the original which stood here a millennium ago. The* torii *gates vary in size, but all indicate a shrine nearby, however small* (above left). *At one Kyoto shrine, a fortune-teller has set up his stall* (above right).

Top and centre
Buddha image and calligraphy at temples in Kyoto.

Above
The wooden roof of Higashi-Honganji, one of the most prominent temples in central Kyoto.

Right
The Temple of the Golden Pavilion, monastic retreat in Kyoto of the great 14th-century shogun Yoshimitsu. The temple was burned to the ground in 1950 by a deranged priest but rebuilt exactly as before. Yukio Mishima wrote a famous novel, also called The Temple of the Golden Pavilion, *about this incident.*

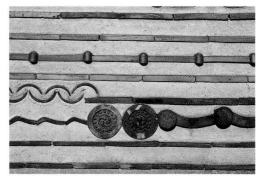

The gardens of Kyoto's Zen temples, some formed of rocks and shrubs, some merely of rocks, moss and gravel, are among the most celebrated products of the Japanese imagination. Decorations on the outer wall of Kyoto's Daitokuji Temple (left centre) reveal a similarly sophisticated taste for abstract design.

Autumn in Kyoto: at Katsura Detached Palace (above), and perhaps the most beautiful example of Japanese domestic architecture; at Sanzen-In (left) and Manshu-In (below left) temples, and on the great butai (scaffold) of Kiyomizu Temple (right).

Left
Participants in Kyoto's Gion Matsuri, held in July, perhaps the single most famous festival in all Japan.

Above
Exterior of a traditional restaurant in Kyoto.

Right
A little restaurant selling condiments on the side.

Left
Despite its reputation for tranquility and elegance, Kyoto has a nightlife which can be as raucous as that of any other Japanese city.

Top
Weaving is one of Kyoto's most venerable trades.

Above centre, above and right
Houses and shops in Kyoto's backstreets.

Castles such as this famous one at Osaka may be seen all over Japan. They were the centres of power of local lords.

Above

The Daibutsu — Great Buddha — of Todaiji Temple in Nara. Fifteen metres (53 feet) in height, it took eight attempts before it was successfully cast. The 'eye-opening' ceremony in 752 AD was one of the great events in early Japanese history. Some 10,000 guests attended, including many from overseas; the pupils of the statue's eyes were painted in by a priest from India!

The stone and metal lanterns (left and right) are at Kasuga Shrine in Nara. The thatched tea-house (centre), though new, fits well the muted ambience at Nara.

73

Left
Torii *gate of Miyajima Shrine near Hiroshima in the Inland Sea, traditionally one of the 'three most beautiful sights' in Japan. The scenery of the island itself, whose name means 'shrine island', is delightfully pastoral, with beautiful woodlands and tame deer everywhere.*

Above
Hiroshima Castle: the original, constructed in 1589, was destroyed by the atom bomb. This skilful reproduction, although completed in ferro-concrete, retains the elegance of the original.

Right
'Thousand Cranes' origami donated by schoolchildren to a Hiroshima bomb memorial. The note expresses the sentiment 'No More Hiroshimas'.

Top
View of Uwajima, on the Inland Sea coast.

Left
Trams in Matsuyama, on the island of Shikoku, fourth in size of the main islands of Japan.

Petite Matsuyama Castle, just three storeys high, was built in 1602 and is one of the best-preserved in the country. The wooden additions have miraculously survived fire.

Following pages
Nagasaki, the port city in northeast Kyushu founded by Europeans in the 15th century, has many interesting reminders of its cosmopolitan past, including ancient shops selling castella (Portuguese-style sponge cake), the villas of 19th-century Western businessmen and a Russian restaurant. Much of the city was decimated by the atom bomb in 1945 but it has been entirely rebuilt.

AN A TO Z OF FUN FACTS

A

Ainu The original inhabitants of Japan who lived in the northern regions and the island of Hokkaido. The Ainu are a Caucasian race and are believed to have crossed a now submerged land bridge from eastern Siberia. Their descendants today number only a few thousand, most having intermarried.

Architecture Traditional Japanese buildings are made only of wood. For example, the Horyu, a seventh century temple in Nara, is one of the oldest wooden buildings in the world. Another traditional building is the castle, many of which were built of wood and stone in the 15th and 16th centuries. In the early 20th century, architecture followed Western styles and since the 1960s, many earthquake-proof skyscrapers have been built, the largest and most spectacular in Shinjuku, Tokyo.

B

Bonsai Small, stunted trees cultivated by periodic pruning and root cutting. The art of bonsai and bonkei (miniature landscapes) is governed by Japanese ideas of natural beauty and aesthetics.

Bullet Train The English name for Shinkansen (new trunk line). The train runs from Tokyo to Hakata at speeds up to 240 km per hour (145 mi per hour).

C

Capsule hotels These hotels offer sleeping berths and shower facilities for guests. Each capsule room is two metres (six feet) long and one metre (three feet) wide and just high enough to sit up in. The guests must climb ladders to reach their bunks.

Climate Three of Japan's four main islands lie in the temperate zone, but there are significant differences in climate. Okinawa in the south is tropical, whereas Hokkaido in the north is under snow for up to five months of the year. There are four distinct seasons, varying according to the region. The summers are wet with monsoons in June and July. Winters are dry and often cold with snow.

D

Daibutsu The Great Buddha at Nara is 16.2 m (53 ft) high and has thumbs 1.6 m (5 ft) long. He weighs 437 tons. His left hand is big enough to hold a sumo wrestling ring and, during the annual spring clean in August, workers can be seen crawling in and out of his nostrils.

Dejima In 1639, when the third Tokugawa shogun expelled all foreigners from Japan, he allowed a few Dutch traders to remain on a specially constructed island in Nagasaki harbour. The island was completed in 1641 and named Dejima, which literally means Exit Island. Holland kept a small group of traders on the island for the next 213 years.

E

Earthquakes Japan lies on one of the earth's largest and most unstable geological faults. Minor earthquakes occur every day but most are not detectable. The most recent major earthquake was in 1923 resulting in a loss of life of some 100,000 people. Major earthquakes seem to occur approximately every 70 years and if this cycle continues, Japan will face one in the early 1990s.

Edo The old name for Tokyo. Edo means estuary and refers to the village situated at, what is now, the Bay of Tokyo. By the 17th century, the village had acquired a fortress, and had become the fief capital of Ieyasu Tokugawa, who became a shogun in 1603. All his followers and family, about 80,000 of them, moved to Edo, which became a city almost overnight. In 1635 it was decreed that all the feudal lords should build mansions in Edo, thus accelerating its growth.

Emperor Japan's first emperor is believed to have come to power in 660 BC. Before 1945, the emperor was regarded as divine although he had no real power, which for much of Japan's recent history has been in the hands of the shoguns and later the samurai. During the American occupation (1945–50), Emperor Hirohito formally announced that he was not divine.

F

Forget-the-year parties From mid-December until New Year, the Japanese hold forget-the-year parties to forget all the bad things that happened during the year.

Fuji, Mount The national symbol of Japan and the highest point at 3,716 m (12,388 ft). Mount Fuji is located several hundred miles southwest of Tokyo. It is a conical volcano which last erupted in 1707. It is also the national symbol of Japan and is held sacred by the Japanese who attempt to climb to the top once in a lifetime.

G

Geisha The word geisha literally means a talented person. The word was coined in the 17th century to describe the female entertainers, many of whom were also courtesans. The status of the geisha was elevated over the next two centuries as their training became more formal. In the 19th century businessmen and politicians competed to take a famous geisha as a mistress.

Grandmother Throwing-away Mountain A mountain near Nagano where in ancient times poor families took their grandmothers when they could no longer care for them and left them there to die. Today, it is a popular place for moon-viewing.

H

Haiku A highly stylized and refined form of poetry consisting of 17 syllables arranged in three lines of five, seven and five syllables each.

Hosutesu The Japanese rendering of the word hostess. There are an estimated 100,000 hostesses in Japan, serving in the nightclubs and cabarets. The hosutesu are employed to entertain guests to a club, for which the guest pays a (usually high) fee.

Hokkaido The second largest island, located in the north of Japan. Hokkaido makes up 22% of Japan's total land area but has only 5% of the population.

Honshu The largest of the four Japanese islands. All main cities and regions are located on Honshu. It comprises 61% of the total land area of Japan and is larger than England, Scotland and Wales put together. The island has a range of mountains running down the middle, giving it a wealth of volcanoes, gorges and mountainous scenery.

Horyu Temple Built in AD 607, this is the oldest temple in Japan and one of the oldest wooden structures in the world.

I

Ise Training Centre This is a training camp for employees of Japanese companies. The regime is strict and requires participants to undergo rigorous physical exercise, intensive lectures on social obligations, group singing and dancing and a dip in the icy waters of the Isuzu River.

J

Japanese language Japanese is a mixture of northern and southeastern Asiatic languages, but its precise origins have not been positively established. In Japanese there is a rigid rule for word order — subject, object and verb. However there is no difference between singular and plural, no way of expressing gender and no definite or indefinite articles. There are also only two tenses — past and present.

K

Kakushi gei Literally this means hidden talent and refers to some skill such as singing and dancing which the Japanese do not mention but are expected to display at social gatherings.

Kamikaze This word means Divine Wind and refers to the typhoon winds which stopped the attempted Mongol invasions in 1274 and 1281. In the Second World War, fighter pilots were called kamikaze pilots in a reference to these historical occasions.

Kyoto The capital of Japan from 794 to 1868. It is now a famous tourist centre with many temples and shrines and an imperial palace which is still used by the imperial family.

Kyushu The southernmost of Japan's four large islands. Kyushu is considered the centre of Japanese culture. It is extremely mountainous and is home of the world's largest volcano — Mount Aso.

L

Land area The total land area of Japan is 378,000 km² (146,000 mi²).

Life expectancy The Japanese have the highest longevity in the world. Life expectancy for women is 82 years and for men 75 years.

Location Lying off the northeast coast of Asia, Japan is made up of four islands — Hokkaido, Honshu, Shikoku and Kyushu. The islands form a crescent-shaped archipelago which lies between the Sea of Japan and the Pacific Ocean.

M

Mongol invasions Kublai Khan, the first Mongol emperor of China, sent invasion fleets to Japan in 1274 and 1281. On both occasions the Mongol ships were sunk by typhoons. This gave rise to the belief that Japan was divinely protected from invasion.

N

Ninja The secret agents of feudal Japan. The ninja specialized in spying and all skills which enabled them to spy without detection. Many people believed they had magical powers, such as the ability to become invisible. They were often hired by the samurai families to assassinate political rivals.

O

Okinawa The Prefecture of Okinawa is a group of 60 islands which were occupied by the Americans after the Second World War and returned to Japan in 1972. The island of Okinawa is 684 km (425 mi) south of Kyushu and has a population of one million.

P

Population 120 million. Japan is the most densely populated country in the world.

R

Religions The Japanese are said to be 80% Shinto and 80% Buddhist. This is because many Japanese practise both religions. There are also small numbers of Christians in Japan.

Ronin Formerly this word was used to describe a samurai who had lost his master during feudal times. These men became wanderers because other masters would not take them on and they were unsuited to other occupations. Today, the word is used to describe high school graduates who fail the rigorous examinations for university.

S

Sake The rice wine which has been brewed since the beginning of Japanese civilization. At first sake was a gruel which was eaten and was used as an offering to the (Shinto) gods. Its modern liquid form is still used as an offering, but also drunk on non-religious occasions. In sake drinking etiquette it is considered impolite to fill one's own cup.

Sashumi Raw fish eaten alone. If eaten with rice it is called sushi.

Shinto The indigenous religion of Japan. Shinto means the way of the gods. The practice of Shinto involves paying respect to the spirits of all things in nature and one's ancestors. This is the origin of the Japanese love of nature and its beauties. Shinto has no specific dogma or belief system, yet its influence pervades Japanese life.

Stock exchange The Tokyo Stock Exchange is the largest in the world.

Sumo A form of wrestling which is Japan's oldest sport. Sumo wrestlers train for many years and are graded in a strict hierarchy. They are famous for being Japan's largest men, each weighing between 250 and 300 pounds. The aim of sumo wrestling is to throw one's opponent off balance, or throw him out of the ring.

T

Tea ceremony Tea drinking was imported from China by Emperor Shomu (AD 701–56). At first it was drunk only by priests who used it to stay awake during meditation. The tea ceremony was invented by a merchant called Sen-no Rikyu in the 16th century. It was designed to be a simple, spiritually enriching ceremony in which the participants communed with nature. There are now several tea ceremony schools teaching varying rules on how it should be conducted.

Tunnels The Seikan undersea railway tunnel, which links the island of Honshu to Hokkaido, is the longest undersea tunnel in the world. It is 54 km (33.49 mi) long and 236 m (787 ft) below the sea.

U

Unlucky numbers The two unluckiest numbers are four and nine. This is because the Japanese word 'four' sounds like the word for death and the word 'nine' sounds like the word for suffering.

V

Visas Tourist visas are usually available on request and last for 90 days. 45 countries have visa exemption agreements with Japan.

Volcanoes About one tenth of the active volcanoes of the world are located in Japan.

W

Written Japanese Written Japanese is a combination of three systems. A simplified and abbreviated version of Chinese characters was adopted in the eighth century but since these ideograms express only one sound, a system called hiragana is also used to represent individual syllables. Also used is katakana, a kind of shorthand used to spell out foreign words.

Z

Zen A form of Buddhism which was introduced to Japan from China in the 12th century. Zen Buddhism advocates achieving enlightenment through prolonged meditation and strictly disciplined behaviour. These practices were taken up by the samurai and the thinking influenced the samurai code of practice, bushido.

INDEX

Akihabara 27
Akihito, Emperor 16
Aomori 59
Asakusa 4, 17, 20
Ashikaga 17
Atom bomb 77; memorial 75
Autumn 4, 15, 66

Buddha 19; Great Buddha, Kamakura 48; Daibutsu 19, 72
Buddhism 15, 16, 63

Castles 73, 75, 77
Cha-no-yu 18
Cherry-blossom viewing 15, 44
Chidori-ga-fuchi 43
Children's Day 4
China 15, 18
Chinese 16
Christianity 18
Coming-of-Age Day 42
Courtesans 19
Craftsmen 4

Daibutsu 19, 72
Daitokuji Temple 64
Dutch 18
Dyeing 54

Earthquake 15
Edo 19, 52
Europeans 1, 18, 77

Forty-seven Ronin 37
Francis Xavier 18
Fujiwara 17
Fukui 56
Fushimi Inari Shrine 61

Gardens 64, 66
Geisha 17; quarter, Kyoto 4
Gifu Prefecture 4, 54
Gingko trees 18
Ginza 4, 20, 24, 25, 27, 28
Gion 4
Gion Matsuri, Kyoto 69
Golden Pavilion, Temple of the 63

Hachiman 48
Harajuku 20, 43
Heian 16, 18; court 16–17
Heian Shrine 62
Higashi-Honganji 63
Hiroshima 75
Hiroshima Castle 75
Honshu 4, 16, 54
Horyuji 19

Imperial Palace 32
Inland Sea 75, 76

Jesuits 18
Jizo, Buddhist deity 49

Kabuki 19, 31
Kamakura 17, 48; Great Buddha 48
Kamikaze 17
Kana 25
Kanazawa 19
Kanji 25
Kanto 17
Kasuga Shrine 73
Katsura Detached Palace 66
Kendo 17
Khublai Khan 15, 17
Kimono 17, 24
Kitano Temmangu Shrine 60
Kiyomizu 60
Kiyomizu Temple 4, 61, 66
Koinobori, carp streamers 4
Korea 15
Koto 4, 17
Kura, storehouse 59
Kyoto 4, 16, 17, 52, 60, 62
Kyudo 17
Kyushu 16, 17, 18, 77

Love poetry 16

Magome 52
Mansu-In 66
Marunouchi 24
Matsushima 59
Matsuyama 76
Matsuyama Castle 77

Meiji Emperor 34
Meiji Shrine 20, 34–7, 42
Minamoto clan 17
Minzoku Mura 4
Mishima, Yukio 63
Mitsubishi 24
Miyajima Shrine 75
Momiji, Japanese maple 4
Mongols 17
Mount Fuji 49
Murasaki Shikibu 17

Nagano 50, 51, 52
Nagasaki 18, 77
Nagoya 18
Nara 16, 73
Nara Period 19
Narai 51, 52
New Year 38
Nijubashi Gate 32
Nikko 47
Noh 18, 19
Noren 32

O-ikoshi 41
O-mikuji 38
O-muchi 36
O-sembe 20
Obon 16
Oda Nobunaga 18
Osaka 73

Pachinko 57
Peace Memorial, Nagasaki 19
Portuguese 18, 77
Postmen 16
Religion 16
Restaurants 28, 31, 69
Rice 59
Romaji 25
Ronin, forty-seven 36
Russians 19
Ryokan 52

Sake 20
Samurai 17
Sanja Festival 17
Sanja Matsuri 41
Sanzen-In 66
Sarariman 44
Sea of Japan 19, 56

Seijin-no-Hi 17
Sendai 59
Setsubun 55
Shamisen 19
Shibuya 31
Shichi-go-san Festival 38
Shikoku 76
Shinjuku 20, 24
Shinkansen 13
Shinto 16, 17, 34, 48; priests 36; shrines 35, 38, 62
Shogun 17, 18
Shrine drum 4
Sofukuji Temple 18
Spas 54
Stock exchange 25
Sudare 31

Taira clan 17
Takayama 4, 54
Tea 18; ceremony 18
Tea house 73
Teenagers 31, 43
The Tale of Genji 17
Three most beautiful sights 59
Todaiji 16, 73
Tokugawa Ieyasu 18, 47
Tokugawa shogun 47
Tokyo 15, 24–45
Torii 34, 61, 62, 75
Toshogu Shrine 47
Toyotomi Hideyoshi 18
Trams 76
Tsumago 16, 52

Ukiyoe 19
Uwajima 76

Weaving 54, 71
Weddings 34
Westernization 19, 20

Yakitori 27
Yamato 16
Yokohama 15
Yoritomo, leader of Taira 17, 48
Yoshimitsu, shogun 63
Yoshiwara 19

Zen 17, 18, 64